I0423062

Copyrighted 2016 All rights reserved
M. Rothmiller
Illustrations courtesy of Classroomclipart.com

No copyrighted part of this book may be used or reproduced without
expressed written permission of M. Rothmiller except in the case of
brief quotations embodied in critical articles or reviews. Thank you,
Professor Hogan.

ISBN-10-1539852369
ISBN-13: 978-1539852360

THE ABC's WITH ANIMALS AND PROFESSOR HOGAN.

Hi Kids! I'm Professor Hogan.

The Most Intelligent Dog in the World!

Let's learn the ABC's

A a

A is for Antelope.

B

B b

B is for Bear.

C

C c

C is for Cat.

D

D d

D is for Dog.

E

E e

E is for Elephant.

F

F f

F is for Fox.

G

G g

G is for Gorilla.

H

H h

H is for Hawk.

I

I i

I is for Impala.

J

J j

J is for Jackal.

K

K k

K is for Kangaroo.

L

L l

L is for Lion.

M

M m

M is for Moose.

N

N n

N is for Newt

O o

O is for Owl.

P

P p

P is for Porcupine.

Q

Q q

Q is for Quail.

R

R r

R is for Raccoon.

S

S s

S is for Stork.

T

T t

T is for Tiger.

U

U u

U is for Uakari.

V v

V is for Vulture.

W w

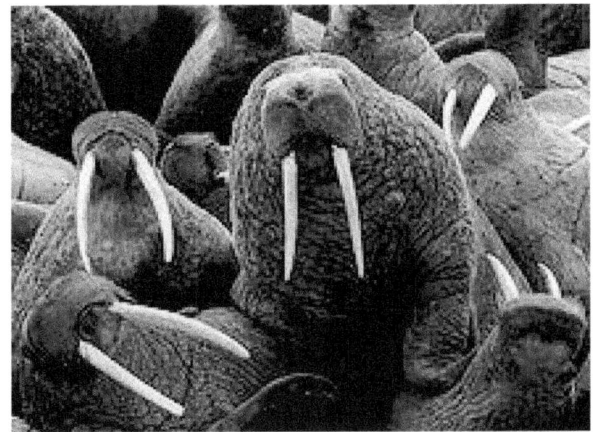

W is for Walrus.

X

W w

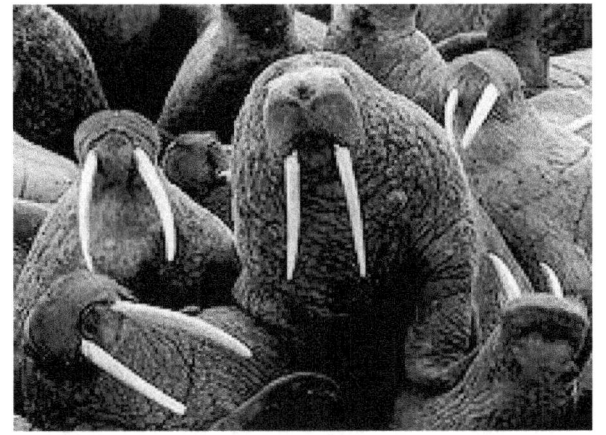

W is for Walrus.

X

X x

X is for Xantus Hummingbird.

Y

Y is for Yak.

Z

Z z

Z is for Zebra.

Very Good!

Now Let's Say the
ABC's Again.

A B C D

E F G H

I J K L

M

N O P Q

R S T
U
V W X
Y
Z

THAT WAS FUN!
SEE YOU SOON.
YOUR FRIEND,
PROFESSOR HOGAN.

GOODBYE

www.ingramcontent.com/pod-product-compliance
Lightning Source LLC
Chambersburg PA
CBHW060222290526
45789CB00003B/1379